HonorSociety.org Scam Watch:

10 Ways to Spot Real or Fake Emails

Mike Moradian

Copyright © 2020 by Mike Moradian

All rights reserved. No part of this book may be used or reproduced by any means, graphic, electronic, or mechanical, including photocopying, recording, taping, or by any information storage retrieval system, without the written permission of the publisher except in the case of brief quotations embodied in critical articles and reviews.

CONTENTS

Tip #2: Do Not Click the Links 3
Tip #3: Scan for Spelling Errors 3
Tip #4: Look for Personal Information Requests 3
Tip #5: The Offer is Unrealistic 3
Tip #6: You Never Initiated the Email 3
Tip #7: The Email Requests You Send Money 3
Tip #8: The Message Contains Some Kind of Threat 3
Tip #9: The Email Claims to be From a Bank or Government Agency 3
Tip #10: Your Gut Tells You Something is Wrong 3
Tip #1: Look for the Display Name 1

A Message from Our Founder: Mike Moradian

More Internet hackers, scammers, and phishing experts than ever before are flocking to email today in an effort to obtain personal information, bank account information, or identification information that can ruin a person's life. With the continual release of new technology, AI, and other automated tools that can make it easy for someone to send fake emails, over and over again, singular attackers are able to impact thousands of students, applications, job-seekers, and graduates today.

Just look at this statistic, for example: phishing attacks grew by 162% between 2010 and 2014. On average, these attacks cost organizations around the world $4.5 billion every single year, with over 50% of internet users receiving at least one phishing email per day. Despite software and other safety walls that are designed to keep phishing emails from landing in your inbox, at the rate at which these hackers are refining their technology, some still manage to slip through.

Naturally, individuals looking for scholarships, information from college admission's boards, responses from organizations or places of employment, and other acceptance letters are going to be at risk for opening a phishing email that promises an answer to one of these questions. It's inevitable.

Our Duty Here at HonorSociety.org

As the founder of HonorSociety.org, an academic honor society that works to advance the positioning and education of our members, helping with everything from professional information and job placements, to scholarships, I feel it is my duty to equip all students and job-seekers out there with the awareness they need to be protected in today's phishing world.

Personally working as internet entrepreneur, founding CampusBuddy and CollegeBudget in addition to HonorSociety.org, I know what lurks in the e-commerce waters for any kind of company today. I have to work daily on the defense against these attackers, just as much as I work on the offense to develop new outreach strategies. HonorSociety.org is no different – except with this platform, it's one that can put hard-working students, job-seekers, and graduates at risk.

That brings us to this e-book, where I am going to look at 10 ways for you to easily spot a real or fake email. If you are reading this, you have probably already received a phishing email in your inbox, at some point, that you knew was fake. Many emails are obviously fake. But, with each passing day, these attackers are becoming more sophisticated, which means that "fake" line is becoming harder and harder to identify.

HonorSociety.org Email Scam Alerts is going to cover clever ways in which you can truthfully decide if you are dealing with a real or fake email by the time you complete our checklist, as well as a few tips for knowing if an email is, indeed, real.

Remember: your personal information, ID, and bank account information can be at risk if you are not careful with these phishing emails, which is why it's wise to go through your inbox each day clear headed and with time set aside to properly look over each email.

Let's get started. You have no time to lose!

TIP #1:

Look for the Display Name

One of the first things you notice about a fresh new email in your inbox is the display name. This is otherwise known as the name that appears next to the email address, often outlined in brackets. These names are then organized into a vertical top down structure that makes it easy for you to sift through emails, organize notices, and process dozens of email at a time.

The display name can be different from the email, as well as the same. Generally, if a legitimate person emails you from, let's say, Morgan Stanley, the display name and address are going to line up. The display name would be "Morgan Stanley" and the email would probably be "contact@morganstanley.com."

However, this is one of the quickest ways to know if you are dealing with a phishing artist. One company, Return Path, analyzed more than 760,000 email threats that targeted 40 of the world's largest brands. They found that nearly 50%

of the attackers spoofed the brand in the display name, which is good news for you.

Here's where this can get tricky.

Different Display Names Can Sneak Through Malware

If you have basic malware or anything of the sorts set up on your computer, it's going to work overtime to try and block out everything that is lacking in legitimacy. But, if a phishing artist uses an email like "contact@ourbank.com" but pairs it up with a display name that says Jim's Scholarship Fund, then the email is going to appear legitimate and sneak through.

Why?

Because you might already have Jim's Scholarship Fund blocked by your malware. But since the email is different from the name, it's still going to display in your inbox, and probably look legitimate.

Don't Trust the Display Name

It's good practice to check every single display name that lands in your inbox. If anything remotely looks suspicious, do not open the email. If you spot any inconsistency in a display name lining up with an email address, do not open the email.

Don't Forget This Domain Name Trick

We're going to look at another trick that should hopefully position you strategically out of the starting gates. You don't need to be a DNS naming structure expert to understand how to spot a phishing artist today. Remember that the last part of a domain name is always the most telling. Take this email for example: "info.alexsharp.com." That email is the child domain of "alexsharp.com." Since alexsharp.com appears on the right-hand side, that is how you can tell the legitimacy.

But, if you get an email like alexsharp.maliciousdomain.com, placing the domain on the left-hand side now, it is clear this email did not originate from the parent email, as outlined above.

Phishing artists constantly try this trick as a way to convince victims that a message is coming from a company like Apple, by sending related emails like "Appleinfo.contacttoday.com." Unless the domain is direct, to the point, with the contacting agency's name as the right-hand part of the email, that is another way to spot a fraudulent attack.

With these two tricks, it should be easier for you to spot mismatched names and domains, as well as fraudulent domains related to real, legitimate platforms.

Of course, we can't spot everything, or necessarily tell if every email is fraudulent in this manner, which is why sometimes, you might end up clicking open the email. Fear not – these emails will require you to click on some kind of link or attachment in order for them to steal your personal information.

The interior of the email should be able to help you confirm your sneaking suspicions, which is what we're going to look at next.

TIP #2:

Do Not Click the Links

At the end of the day, the ultimate goal of a phishing email, besides asking for credit card or bank account information, is to get you to click on a malicious link. This link can then send a virus into your computer that can phish for personal login credentials, as well as do a slew of other things. Some of these links can go directly into your email inbox and start scanning your emails for critical information related to applications and so forth, like your Social Security Number.

That's why it's so important to never, ever click the links in phishing emails. We understand you might end up opening the emails by accident. But ALWAYS be weary of email links embedded into already sketchy emails that promise to bring you somewhere for something you have won.

How can you identify if a link is fraudulent in an email? Here are a few precautionary steps to take:

- Hover your mouse over any links embedded into the body of the email.

- Review the link address generated by your mouse. If it looks weird, do not click on it.
- If you are unsure, open a new window and type the link into a browser. Use an Incognito Window to be safe.
- See where the link goes. It should be pretty obvious immediately.

Knowing the Two Types of URLs

Keep in mind, there are two kinds of URLs you can view today:

- Standard-length URL, starting with www, followed by the website name, and ending with a top-level domain.
- Shortened URL, such as goo.gl/V4jVrx.

How can I tell if a link is sketchy? Well, we all know what normal links look like: google.com, honorsociety.org, Walmart.com... you get the picture. If the link is 100 characters long, full of tons of numbers and weird symbols, lacking in a normal ".org or .com" ending, or related to a website name that has nothing to do with the company name or email, it's probably not a link you want to click on.

Naturally, when it comes to the shortened links, however, it can be harder to tell. These do not look like normal links, and can bring you just about anywhere. Phishers are smart and they know this, which is why they will try and hit you with a shortened link where possible. Here is where the next step comes into the picture.

Again, if you are unsure, go to your browser and open an Incognito Window. These are windows that are unrelated to your plugged in accounts, passwords, etc. that you normally use. Typing out the address will remove the link it contains in your email that can then embed itself into your computer. You can safely search the link this way and see what comes up.

Generally, this should be a practice that you do for just about every email, no matter where it comes from.

Sites That Help Detect Scam Links

If you want to be proactive about your link-opening, here are a few sites that will tell you about the integrity of a link immediately:

- KasperSky VirusDesk: This is a dual-purpose tool that checks links to dodgy websites, as well as suspicious files. To use it, simply enter the URL into the site and click "scan." It will immediately tell you what it thinks.
- ScanURL: This independent website takes your link and checks them via a secure HTTPS connection. The tool polls Google Safe Browsing, PhishTank, and Web of Trust to verify the link. If the results list is dangerous, obviously, don't click the link.
- PhishTank: This site is more concerned with phishing sites than it is malware. Enter in the URL. If the URL has already been entered into their tank, they'll tell you immediately. But if it

has not, then you'll get a tracking number. It's worth waiting. As their website says, it can be harder to find out information on phishing emails over plain scamming emails given their fleeting nature.

If there's anything to get from this specific chapter, basically, it's to: never click on the links embedded in a phishing email. Additionally, hackers are going to try and use shortened links where possible since their legitimacy is harder to detect.

If you think about it, most regular email correspondence does not require you to click on a link to arrive at the necessary information. It's already stated.

TIP #3:

Scan for Spelling Errors

This could arguably be the easiest way to spot a phishing email today. However, do note that spelling errors happen, and that regular agencies can indeed include them in their emails. But, it's not likely. Professional settings require proofreading of emails, as well as approvals, which means any spelling error is much more likely to be caught in this kind of vicinity.

Phishing artists, on the other hand, are many times isolated actors that had no one helping to proofread their emails. In many cases, they are located in other countries, which means they do not have an adept understanding of the English language. Since submitting these kinds of emails to proofreaders online can implicate these attackers for who they really are, they are left sending out their typos within their phishing emails.

If you notice one, two, or even more spelling errors, you probably have your answer.

Don't Forget About Grammar

Perhaps everything is spelled correctly – that's easy today with spell check tools. But not even grammarly.com can catch all grammar and regular chat. If you notice that sentences are written in an odd way no regular English speaker would use, that's a good indication the writer was not from one of these big and reputable companies.

Sure, you can use grammarly.com and other sites to check the grammar if you so choose. But generally, in this instance, your gut should be able to tell you if you are reading normal, or odd, prose in an email.

One last tip is entering a "weird sounding sentence" into Google and asking if the correct grammar is being used. Typically, the search engine can provide you with its own grammar check and let you know if your suspicion is correct.

If you are not the greatest speller or wordsmith, don't be afraid to have your friends look over emails that give you a bad feeling. You always want to be sure.

TIP #4:

Look for Personal Information Requests

This one might sound obvious, too, but you'd be surprised how many people end up giving out credit card or account information by accident through a phishing email. We all end up on auto pilot every now and then – it's hard not to given how busy life is for the average person in 2019. We get up, open our emails, and respond to them half asleep in bed as we get the day moving. Before we have even had our morning coffee, we find ourselves answering correspondence that might just ask for something as simple as a credit card expiration date or security code we "inputted incorrectly."

If the email name looks legitimate, like it's coming from Square or PayPal, then we go ahead and do it without second thought.

Well, in this chapter, we're going to look at why it's very important that you still consider the information you are just freely sending out into the internet. There are bad guys in every dark corner of the internet, just waiting for someone to be a little lenient with their personal identification information!

Never Give Up Personal Information

No matter how legitimate an email might appear, there is never a right time to give up personal information. Think about this from a common sense angle:

- Your bank does not need you to confirm your bank account information or credit card information. They already have it. In fact, they are the ones that created this information and assigned it to you in the first place.
- Your recent purchases do not need you to submit your credit card information for a second time. If you have a confirmation email that the order was placed, then trust us, your information went through. The company does not need you to send your information in an email.
- The government does not need you to send personal information like SS numbers in an email. They can go retrieve that information if they really need it.

Look for Obvious Scam Information

If you receive an email asking you to confirm your address, that could be legitimate. Your address is public knowledge and accessible online for anyone who wants it.

Look for these sketchier direct requests, which should send off a red alert:

- Passwords
- Account information
- Bank account information
- Identification information like passport numbers
- Information to other accounts unrelated to the one in question

Remember: most companies understand that information in emails is at risk. Plenty of email viruses go around each year that almost guarantee someone else has read your emails. Look at politicians, for example. Emails can quickly become public sources of information as needed. That's why no agency or company will ever ask you to submit sensitive information in an email. Instead, they have an encrypted portal for credit card number information. They don't want you to be hacked using their services – you'll never shop from them again! Consequently, they will go out of business.

Therefore, if one of these companies needs personal information, like PayPal needing you to verify a transfer, then they are going to do it from within their site, or send an email letting you know about it and prompting you to login. They will not ask that you confirm this information directly in an email.

Basically, there is never an instance when someone is going to ask you to impart personal information in an email. In a rare case in which a company is unprofessional and does so, consider picking up the phone and calling them to confirm the request. Otherwise, make it part of your normal email etiquette to never impart information that can impact your personal and financial future.

TIP #5:

The Offer is Unrealistic

Trust us – we want free things just as much as the next person. It's innate to all human beings – nothing is more appealing than being told you just won a million dollars from a contest you never entered. That's why we buy lotto tickets, spend millions at casinos, and enter giveaway contests on social media just about every day. Winning something for free, or something that will change your future, like a scholarship, is a dream come true.

That's why when we receive an email promising this dream, it can be hard for us to immediately look away. Phishers know this, which is why they pander to your childlike wonder by sending you an offer that is unrealistic.

By now, we all know how life works. Life isn't easy for anyone, which is why if something seems too good to be true, most times it is. No one is going to send you a million dollars for no reason. You are going to need to apply to some program, express interest somewhere, and verify yourself, as well as prove your worth. You will never just have thousands of dollars dropped onto your lap. It's just not how life works.

Therefore, your gut is going to tell you when an offer is unrealistic.

Tips for Spotting Unrealistic Emails

We're going to explore these tips further in coming chapters, but here are a few ways to spot unrealistic emails:

1. **You received something that you did not apply for.** If you did not apply for a scholarship, why would you receive one in your inbox? That's not how it works today. You need to proactively express interest in something if you expect to hear back from the company or agency. They are not going to award random people with money "just because." That would make no sense, nor bode well for the company.

2. **You did not have to exert yourself in any way.** As we mentioned above, life is challenging, which is why nothing worth having ever comes easy. If you want to earn free money or a scholarship, you are going to need to exert yourself in some way. You might need to make an account somewhere, write an essay, fill out a form, etc. You need to, in some capacity, prove that you are worthy of that money.

3. **The offer requires you to click on a link to receive it.** If the email requires you to click on a link to obtain whatever it is that it's promising, step away. Remember: if you applied for a scholarship somewhere and won it, the email is going to tell you everything you need to know. It probably won't require you to click on any link, but rather, respond to the email in the inbox. There is just no need to go to some foreign platform somewhere.

4. **The offer is vague and requires you to click on a link before it tells you anything else.** If the offer is so vague that you really don't know what you just won, chances are, it's a phishing virus. Again, you will be prompted to click on the link to find out what you did win, which makes no sense.

5. **The offer is outrageous, like $20,000 or more.** Sure, there are probably offers this large floating around the internet somewhere. However, they are unlikely, which means receiving notification of winning 100k is not going to make any sense. Phishers are pandering to your hope that you just won some life-changing amount of money, which is why they are going to make the offer outrageous. They aren't concerned with being reasonable. They are using a shock-tactic to elicit a response.

The next time an email tells you you're the new owner of a Porsche, understand that it's probably not true. It's definitely mean that scammers play into this kind of excitement and hope to get you to click on a link, no doubt. But once you understand it's the lay of the land today, you will realize that every "free" email is fake – and it will no longer upset you as much.

We are going to explore a topic we just discussed here further, given its importance in the following chapter.

TIP #6:

You Never Initiated the Email

This is a tricky but important topic for us to cover. By definition, honor societies are an exception to this rule because they initiate the first contact with you. Honor societies generally have partnerships in place with organizations such as universities in order to identify and select eligible members. Keep that in mind when reviewing an honor society invitation, and remember it may be an exception to this general rule.

As we mentioned earlier, if you never initiated an email, why should you be receiving one, out of the blue, making all of these amazing and grandeur promises? If you receive an email with a subject line "Congratulations!!! You won our lottery!!" this should raise some suspicions. If you never entered the lottery in the first place, then how can you be a big lottery winner?

The same holds true for scholarships and other things that we all hope to win in this lifetime.

Here are common emails that might convince you to click on a link, of which you never even applied:

- **Lottery:** We all want to win the lottery. If we did, all of our life's worries and woes would fade into the sands of time. It's the ultimate dream. That's why we can't help but buy the scratch-offs at the local gas station from time to time. Well, with the internet today, there are a variety of lottery-style contests you can enter (although we don't recommend it). If you receive an email claiming you are the winner of some kind of lottery, if you never even bought a ticket, how can that be? And if you are playing online lotteries, then be sure to be very, very careful about the contact you receive from the lottery agency.
- **Scholarships:** College can be downright impossible to fund today, with Forbes estimating that collectively, students carry $1.5 trillion in debt as of 2019. That's why so many students and parents are considering scholarships. There are thousands of them out there, with too many students failing to apply for these niche opportunities. However, if you never applied for a certain scholarship, but receive an email that you miraculously were the winner, that should be a red flag. To get a scholarship, you will need to exert yourself in some way. Generally, you will need to write an essay on some topic proving that you are deserving of this specific scholarship. Here at HonorSociety.org, we can help you apply and

manage scholarship applications, which means we will work as a third party intermediary that keeps you on-track and protected from solicited phishing emails.

- **All-Expense Paid Trips:** Great – you just won a 7-day cruise in the Caribbean for two. But wait, did you ever apply to be the winner? Probably not. Therefore, don't click on the link to redeem your winnings.

- **Grants:** Grants are a great way to get projects moving on behalf of the government. Local governments are allocated a certain amount of funds every year that often go unused. Applying for grants is one of the smartest things you can do, especially for a niche business or project. Just remember: if you didn't apply for the grant, you probably didn't win it. There is only X amount of grant money allocated each year, which means at the very least, you need to apply and you need to fill out some form stating why you should receive it.

- **Loans:** Loans are a natural part of life, which is why so many scammers will try to use them to get you to click on a link. Again, if you didn't apply for the loan on your own, or through a bank or credit agency, why are you now the recipient of the loan? It just doesn't add-up.

- **Giveaways:** This one can be tricky because social media is full of so many legitimate giveaways today. They have become a requirement for brands and individuals that want to remain competitive. If you receive an email about being the winner of a giveaway, first ask yourself if you 1) applied at all and 2) how you applied. If you applied on Instagram by commenting on a post, then you should receive your notice there. If you applied through Facebook Messenger, then you should receive it there. In some cases, you do apply with an email, which is why you should use our other tips to ensure it's a legitimate email.

One great tip is to keep a running log of all the things you apply to on a given basis. You can track applications, contests, lotteries, and giveaways, so you can know exactly what you did and did not apply to. This is a great way to ensure you are never tricked by this kind of phishing email.

TIP #7:

The Email Requests You Send Money

Why on earth would any company require you to send them money before they give you something in return? Sure, memberships require money and so do contests. But you provide that money, every single time, on a website, through an encrypted portal that was intended for it. Never, ever will a company request that you expose your credit card information in an email. Companies are smart, and they know the risk they put you at if they require a credit card expiration date in any ole' email.

Don't Forget Fyre Festival

Fyre Festival became a worldwide sensation in 2017 when this big, outlandish, and luxury-style music festival never happened. That's right – people showed up to this deserted island in the Bahamas, only to discover no stages, no tents, no running water, no nothing. They had been promised everything from private cabanas by the beach while famous artists played in the distance, to seafood, fruit, and drinks hand-delivered to their tents.

In 2019, both Netflix and Hulu put out documentaries that covered this disastrous meltdown, detailing how the scammer behind the madness, Billy McFarland, was able to pull it off (well, until he went to jail). As things started to get dire, he had the Fyre Festival account send out emails to those that had already bought tickets. The email asked everyone to deposit $300 into their Fyre Festival account before arriving to the festival.

This should have had a lot more people shaking their heads. Why on earth would a festival need everyone to front $300? Well, it was because of the massive bankruptcy happening behind closed doors. They needed that money to simply make it to the next step that never happened. The bottom line is no company should ever ask you for money, period.

Money Funnel Attempts

Smarter phishers won't ask for money outright, but they will at some point in their phishing funnel. Here are the different points in which you can be asked to send money:

1. **The Initial Contact Email:** This one is the most aggressive and the most obvious. If an email asks you to outright send money right away, that should be a massive red flag that anyone can spot. Why would any legitimate company ask for your personal credit card information

in an email, much less ask for any money at all? As we mentioned, smart phishers know to wait for their prey.

2. **The First Page of the Virus Link:** In some cases, the email will ask you to click on a link to arrive at your winnings. If you click the link and end up at the landing page, to finally receive your winnings, you might be asked to input your personal contact information. This is the most common way for phishers to casually ask for your credit card information. It seems more normal, too, to be entering it on a site as opposed to inside an email.

3. **Follow Up Correspondence:** Maybe this phisher allows you to "claim your prize" without asking for any money. You click the link, insert your name, and wait. At this point, they may send another email claiming you can't secure your winnings until you enter in a legitimate credit card. This is one other popular way to get you to "without thinking" give over that information.

This is why it's so important to never go into auto pilot mode when going through your emails in the morning. We are so used to inputting card info on sites like Amazon.com, etc. that it can seem like just another normal day if you're doing it for an email you glance over at 7AM. Plus, for people with automatic password filling software on their computer that "remembers your password" and credit card information for you, be extra careful to ensure it doesn't infill your information without you even realizing it.

Don't let autopilot take over when it comes to your personal finances. That is, after all, what these phishers want more than anything – your money.

TIP #8:

The Message Contains Some Kind of Threat

Y ou might be thinking: what phishers would also dare elicit a threat as they try to steal my information and money? You'd be surprised. Much like presenting you with a present gets you to act in some way, so does a potential threat. None of us like to "get into trouble." We don't want to be scolded, or possibly cause some kind of account dilemmas if we fail to sign up for a new package, provide up-to-date information, etc.

Phishers know this, which is why contrary to offering you a present, they will threaten to take away a present if you don't do something immediately. This is an easy way to get you to pay attention to an email in your inbox, especially if the subject line reads something like this "Warning: account deactivation imminent unless we hear from you." It's hard to skip over that, right?

But think about it – when was the last time a company like Walmart sent you any kind of email that threatened you or used the word warning? Never because that's not normal customer service policy. They want you to want to shop on their website, which is why they are always going to be polite and courteous to you. No account shutdown will ever be imminent. No threats will ever be emailed your way.

Still, even though we know that, we can't help but get upset over emails promising some kind of threat.

Here are the most common types of threatening emails phishers send today:

- **Account warning or suspension.** If you get an email stating that your account is about to be suspended if you don't do XYZ, that should be a red flag. Companies are normally going to send you 15 different emails telling you of an upcoming renewal before they terminate an account. In many cases, they would never terminate your account, because they would lose you as a client. The only thing that can get tricky is an account suspension email that could be possible through a site like etsy.com if you violate community standards. But in this case, still, there would be no sketchy link for you to click. It would simply state what happened, and request that you wait a 30-day period or call a provided number.
- **Account termination imminent.** Again, a company is going to tell you at least 15 times before an account is terminated. If your card expired and you are no longer paying the monthly premium, they are going to do

everything they can before they have to terminate your account. They are going to be so annoying, in fact, that it will be hard to ignore. Therefore, any random "your account is being terminated" emails out of the blue should be a phishing indicator.

- **Personal information was exposed through our site.** Sometimes, companies are breached and information is exposed. It can happen. If this is the case, the company will let users know politely and require zero contact. They will not ask you to click on a link. They will brief you on the situation, what could have been exposed, and what you should do now. Generally, they will request that you change login information, your bank account password, etc. They will NOT request that you do anything with them or provide them with any amount of this information.

- **Unauthorized login attempt.** Companies do alert users if someone is trying to hack into your account, it's true. They will not embed a sketchy link into the email to tell you this. They will alert you to the situation and ask you to reset your username and password. Do this independently of any link they send. Go to the site by typing it in and view your account without visiting it directly through a link. This is a hard one to spot, which is why it's best if you go around the virus and simply type it in yourself.

No normal business pursues a threatening marketing tactic. That's a quick way to ensure your doors are closed. Just remember that piece of common sense you might forget as a phishing email "guilts" you into an action you otherwise wouldn't consider.

TIP #9:

The Email Claims to be From a Bank or Government Agency

N o one wants to get in trouble with the government, which is why phishers will try and mimic the government in emails to people. The most common government-related scam of the last few years has been scammers trying to get older people to send in personal information related to collecting their social security checks. Since these people did not have scammers or phishing artists back in their day, they are presently not aware of the advanced tools and tricks these people can leverage at a moment's notice today.

Pretending to be a bank or a government agency can be a tough phishing campaign to crack. It's certainly one of the more advanced angles that can get people from time to time, which is why you need to follow along with our trips below for remaining vigilant despite the attacks:

1. Think Back to Our Display Name Tips:

This is going to come in handy with this kind of phishing. This is where you can see if the URL is indeed irs.gov or if it's something like irs.collectionsandinsurance.com. The latter is a false email that has messed with the right-hand side of the URL, indicating its irrelevance. The same holds true for big-time banks and other collection agencies. It's common for phishers to try and be:

- The IRS
- The FBI
- Local collection agencies
- Social security

2. Remember: Our Government Agencies Don't Contact You Via Email:

This might not be the case for people living outside the U.S., but it's certainly the case for people who do live here. The IRS is not going to send you a personal email as their initial point of contact if something is wrong. They are going to send you a letter or call you. It's how our official agencies do business in the U.S. Therefore, most times, any email or text claiming to be a government agency is going to be false. We understand if you still want to open it just to be sure.

3. All Personal Information is Inputted Directly Via Website:

Any sensitive information that a bank needs from you is going to be inserted into their website through their encrypted portal. They are not going to ask you for it through an email. Government agencies, especially, already have this information – they are the ones that assign you personal IDs and driver's licenses, etc. It should seem odd if they are asking you to supply such information out of the blue.

4. Did You Do Anything Wrong?

If the "IRS" contacts you in December about a tax return you completed 3-years ago, think about that relevance. You should only be contacted by agencies that make sense. If you have never done anything wrong, why is the FBI on your case? Much like our lottery example above, that same principle holds true for government agencies and banks hunting you down. Many times, phishers will pretend to be banks you don't even do business with!

The bottom line is that government agencies and banks act with professionalism in our country. They will not contact you personally through email regarding an urgent matter. They will call you or send you a letter, which is why you want to tread very lightly with any emails claiming to need sensitive government data immediately.

TIP #10:

Your Gut Tells You Something is Wrong

Every single human being has something called an intuition. This is a little voice inside your head that tells you if it thinks something is wrong or right. It's a personal dialogue you can have with yourself, right inside your head, at any point during the day. Many times, we don't even realize when we are talking to our gut instincts, which is why we can fail to listen to our natural inclination and get ourselves in trouble.

This intuition is the product of your learned and unlearned behavior. It's attached to your subconscious, which is a deeper level of your mind that is constantly absorbing information around it – even while you sleep. This subconscious comes to develop a mind of its own, that in many times, is more accurate that your conscious mind. Your conscious mind is impacted by your experiences, likes, dislikes, and opinions, which means it can be wrong.

Your subconscious, the other hand, is merely learned behavior from all the things you see and consume every day. It's more impartial, and therefore, something you should listen to when it pipes up.

Listen to Your Heart (Gut)

We all have a grandmother that tells us to follow our gut. It's what makes us unique and reactive. Well, this same response holds true for phishing emails. When you receive an email that you feel just quite isn't right, that's your gut telling you something is wrong. How does your gut know? Your subconscious has probably scanned over 10,000 emails at this point in your life, which means it knows a thing or two about normal email structure. It also knows a thing or two about normal chit-chat, and what is customary for outreach on behalf of a company, government, agency, and so forth.

If you feel this little tingling sensation in your chest or stomach start to flutter when you look at a new email in your inbox, that's your gut already telling you something is off. Many times, it's hard to even describe what exactly is "off." That's what's so impressive about our intuitions. It can be simply:

- **Tonality:** Your gut knows when someone's tone is a little off. Email can make this hard since written correspondence has removed the natural emotions and expressions of talking in-person. But your gut can still, nevertheless, spot a fake tone – which exists in every kind of phishing email. There is nothing genuine behind it!

- **Grammar:** Your gut also knows normal, casual English grammar. It can immediately tell if some kind of phisher has drafted the email it is scanning. Your gut can even tell this before your conscious eyes have laid eyes on it reading.
- **Style:** This can include bold, italics, punctuation, etc. Either way, your gut can form an opinion on any email in just seconds after reading it.
- **Intention:** Have you ever had a bad feeling about a person you know? Something just tells you that they are up to no good? Your intuition can arrive at the same conclusion from an email, believe it or not. Be sure to listen to it!

You are smarter than you probably give yourself credit for – if you feel this little voice in your head telling you that you are reading a scam, you probably are! Be sure to follow our other 9 steps in this case for identifying if the email is indeed a phishing email, and what you can do to keep your information and passwords safe and protected.

That concludes the 10 tips for spotting phishing emails portion of this e-book. In the final section, we are going to look at additional tips for spotting phishers, how to know when you've uncovered a true email, and what you can do to remain vigilant heading into the future.

Additional Tips for Staying on Top of Phishers

We could go on all day covering the best ways to identify if you have opened up a phishing email. Although we just covered what we believe to be the top 10 most important things to look out for in every email, we are going to cover a few more topics that didn't make the list. We want to provide you with all necessary information to ensure you are prepared and educated with all things cybersecurity.

Our Secondary Phishing Email List

1. **Review the Signature:** If there is no signature, half of a signature, or a signature that does not line up with the email and the header, this is another red flag. Legitimate companies and agencies will always have a proper signature embedded into the email. The lack of one should be an indication of their unprofessionalism.

2. **Do Not Download Attachments:** Some phishers are including physical attachments in their emails as opposed to links. Others are including both. We don't typically associate attachments with viruses, which is why this can be a smart way for them to creep into your personal information. If you suspect that the email is fraudulent, do not download any attachments included with the email.

3. **Study the Salutation:** Does the email address you, personally, or is it vague like "hello valued customer?" It's hard for phishers to try and know your exact name, which is information that any company or agency should have. Therefore, if you receive some anonymous greeting, you should tread with caution.

4. **The Message is Designed to Make You Panic:** If you feel yourself getting nervous from reading an email, chances are, it's a phishing email. They are trying to elicit a certain response out of you, whether it's rooted in fear or motivation. That means the emails are going to get you uncomfortable and feeling like you need to do something immediately, or like you did something wrong. They will not be passive in nature whatsoever.

Legitimate companies are not going to solicit information, money, or threatening responses from you. They are going to spell emails correctly, use passive language, and refrain from attaching random attachments that you "must" download.

Although this can all seem like common sense, it's still important to remain proactive in this digital era we live in today.

Knowing When It's a Real Email: 5 Tips

Now it's time to understand when you are, in fact, dealing with a real email. In some instances, emails do require you to act, perhaps if you didn't submit your taxes correctly, etc. You need to know if an email is real in order to be a productive member of society, which is why we felt it was important to include that in this e-book!

So how can you piece apart the legitimate from the non-legitimate emails? Here are our 5 tips to help:

1. It's An Email You Were Expecting:

This one goes without saying – if you are expecting an email from a company or a specific person, and you receive an email from them, then that's a good indicator it's a true and real email. That's why it's a good idea to keep some kind of contact log or calendar at your disposal where you track all of your correspondence and who has/has not answered you yet. Plus, this is good for staying on top of things that will make your life that much more organized.

2. It's Non-Threatening:

Normally, real emails don't pose a threat to you and your well-being for the day. They are simply meant to extend a conversation or answer a question. If the subject line and body of the email do not threaten account termination, credit card fraud, or dramatic winning announcements, it's probably real.

3. The Right-Hand Side of the Email is Legitimate:

Remember when we talked about email URLs? Make sure to check the right-hand side of the email. If it indeed says, person@apple.com, then you can actually rest assured you are receiving an email from Apple. You can always use the websites we included earlier to still check on the legitimacy of the email if you want!

4. It Just Feels Right:

You've sent thousands of emails in your life. You are more of an expert than you might think! If you can sense that it's a normal, legitimate email, then you are probably right. Remember to listen to that gut feeling in your chest – it's a guiding force that knows more than you give it credit for!

5. It Wasn't Sent at Some Odd Hour:

Many times, phishing emails are sent from overseas, which means they can land in your inbox at 2AM. What normal person is sending out work emails in the middle of the night? General correspondence happens between 8AM and 8PM, which is why you should always look at the email timestamp. If it arrives during regular working hours, it's another indicator that it's actually real. It's important to note that due to common email marketing tools, legitimate e-mails can be sent late at night to tier out sending or to avoid sending too much traffic to a website at the same time. Therefore this rule should be viewed as a general additional suggestion to consider rather than a strict rule.

Practice makes perfect, which means the more you adhere to these rules and suggestions when managing your email inbox, the more confident you will get in your ability to determine fact from fiction.

Parting Words – Stay Vigilant

Cyber attacks, phishing emails, and fraudulent online and mobile activity are on the rise – there's no way around it. Between 2016 and 2017, cyber crime costs [accelerated at 23%](), which is only going to increase as the more recent numbers come in. The accessibility of phones, laptops, and tablets, plus readily available internet and WiFi, makes it easier than ever before for aggressors to try and phish you into their latest scam.

That's why you need to remain vigilant. As we write this e-book, some phishing artists are coming up with new ways to gain your information that we haven't even learned of yet. The good news it that our 10 tips are designed to keep you aware with a heightened sense of vigilance as you go through your inbox, positioning you powerfully no matter what they concoct in the future.

We recommend keeping this checklist next to you when you are at the computer, as a reminder of all of the different things you can do to keep your personal and financial information protected. There is no need to expose yourself to hacking if you just take a moment to reflect on your due diligence and how you can out-smart the phishers.

HonorSociety.org

Here at HonorSociety.org, it's our job to position you as successfully as possible for a lucrative, productive, and accessible future. That's why we want you to be aware of the dangers of email, especially as you wait for that college acceptance, the loan receipt, or any other kind of email that can change your life. Hackers know this, which is why they are going to come in and muddle the waters.

We exist to enhance academic and professional success, which starts with you today. We want you to succeed, connect with other people in your field of study, and create a long-term goals strategy that makes it possible for you to achieve all that you have dreamed of. Driven by our community core values, funded by members just like you, we live to serve each Honor Society participant today.

From career advancement tools, to member discounts and scholarship connections, the world can be your oyster. Remain protected from phishers, scammers, and hackers in the mean-time with our tips imparted here today. If you liked what you read, please feel free to share this e-book with your friends and followers on social media!

We want everyone to be aware of what they are up against. Thanks for reading.

Keywords

HonorSociety.org
Honor Society

Reviews
Wikipedia
Real
Legitimate

www.ingramcontent.com/pod-product-compliance
Lightning Source LLC
Chambersburg PA
CBHW050314220526
45465CB00005B/1988